StrongWords

Voices Of A New Generation

Edited by

Liz Wakefield

First published in Great Britain in 1997 by
STRONGWORDS
1-2 Wainman Road, Woodston,
Peterborough, PE2 7BU
Telephone (01733) 230746
Fax (01733) 230751

HB ISBN 186188 519 9
SB ISBN 186188 514 8

FOREWORD

Although we are a nation of poetry writers we are accused of not reading poetry and not buying poetry books: after many years of listening to the incessant gripes of poetry publishers, I can only assume that the books they publish, in general, are books that most people do not want to read.

Poetry should not be obscure, introverted, and as cryptic as a crossword puzzle: it is the poet's duty to reach out and embrace the world.

The world owes the poet nothing and we should not be expected to dig and delve into a rambling discourse searching for some inner meaning.

The reason we write poetry (and almost all of us do) is because we want to communicate: an ideal; an idea; or a specific feeling.

Poetry is as essential in communication, as a letter; a radio; a telephone, and the main criteria for selecting the poems in this anthology is very simple: they communicate.

In this fast moving world where changes happen dramatically and rapidly, there is often a barrier between different generations we've grown up in what seems like almost two different worlds.

It's hard for each generation to understand the other, but, the younger generation see things differently and form their opinions from today's world - not from the past. *Voices of a New Generation* is an anthology of verse written entirely by the youth of today. Through their poems they have communicated their thoughts, feelings, views and opinions.

This anthology represents 18-25 year olds and everyone who reads it will get an honest and true insight into the minds of youngsters. It breaks down the barriers in communication between generations and lets the youth say exactly what they want without any interference.

CONTENTS

THE WORLD

The world
Full of anger, hate, despair
The world
Full of people that don't seem to care
The world
Where things are getting worse
The world
It seems to be under a curse
The world
Where danger is round every corner
The world
She's in danger, somebody warn her
The world
She's here for us to share
The world
Let's make sure we start to care.

Andrea Preece

MEMOIRS OF THE LOWER SIXTH

The smell of rain and lost values,
Lips and tights -
Grunge subsiding.
Pot noodle warmth,
Ease away heartbreak.

Abbi Lock

TEENAGE ANGST

Feel the central crust and eat,
it's better to know yourself. Sit
and pick the pieces with an ever-present thumbnail,
an elusive blade.
Draw a face on it, become mother,
suck, become baby, break it
become dreamless.
Palms reflect your words, map of face, your story
wearing gloves, as always.
It's better to know yourself.
There's a thin line, age and youth, at least nowadays.
Remember you'll grow out of it, isn't that what
they always say.
Know the flavour of yourself, love it on your teeth,
'cus, hey, age is just a number.
You'll grow up soon.

Maria Walker

ROUTINE

Dry lips scraped my skin,
Your hands ran roughly over my flesh;
Feeling, fondling, taking.
Looked at the ceiling, ignored the pain,
Forced the vomit into the pit of my stomach.

Tonight you need me,
You've had a long day.
'I love you, I want you, my angel.'
Your breath has clouded the window,
I can no longer see my tree;

I could sit all day in my tree,
Let the wind freshen my skin.
This seems sickening;
Your sweat wets my bed.
'I love you, my angel. I know you like it.'

You liked it when others were there
And I had to call you daddy.

Nicole Ansell

EARLY BEDTIME

This sunset, this lonely early bedtime
is where I sit dripping with troubles.
Could I have travelled further to
sacrifice this star?
Travel was my baptism,
My rebirth into the living world.
The creation of a new star to reach,
Without the smears of that old moon.
Here though I sit in an empty well,
Memory is the bedrock of this dreamer.
This new brace is bending.
Do I return and face you?
Or do I just rub these smears in deeper.

Robert Mitchell

Lonely Old Lady In NHS Hospital

He's tottering round on his rounds,
I am doing what I do best,
In the dark, blue hospital room,
White-yellow lamp on, like my skin,
Drips feeding
Bodies sighing
A radio somewhere softly sounding.
She looks at me sometimes.

She glances as she fumbles at nothing,
Every moment it seems a wish.
For what is she asking?
An opening or an ending?

She sings sometimes.
Old songs.
Voice of a child.
Do we forget?
Time to remember her mumbling is real,
Her cries are needs
And time is the reverse.
But through weary eyes she remains.

Natasha

THOUGHTS

Like the sun I'm being replaced by the clouds,
Like the moon I'm on my own,
The stars no longer come out,
The room is empty, the air is cold,
No-one left to share the warmth,
Too late I'm letting go.
I fall down one more time,
No-one's hand reaches out to understand,
I hear someone's voice but it's not yours,
Trying too hard to picture you here,
But it's no good,
Being used to you everyday,
I took you for granted in my own selfish way,
I'll never be able to find a reason for
letting you go,
If you can't understand how I'm feeling,
I guess you'll never know.

Linda Simon

STONE

Eyes narrow,
intolerance is
easy.
- wag a finger
reproachfully
blame them:
lazy, stupid,
good for nothing.
Then stop
condemning.
Take an introspective
look at your
attitude,
- it's twisted,
distorted,
reflects a narrow
view.
Why don't you
widen your horizons
Look further than
your own nose,
see in more ways than
through your own eyes -
you might be surprised.

Anna Langley-Smith

UNDERACHIEVER

Expectation.
Reality.
The two fuse together like a brick and a window.
I'm left with the broken pieces
with which I'm supposed to create an academic career.

Underachiever.
That's me.
'Too busy enhancing my public persona.'
If that's the case
why haven't I got one?

Underachiever.
That's me.
When I do badly I should do well;
When I do well I should do better.
No questions asked.

No recognition.
No reward.
Just a report that tells me my grades are slipping.
A touch of encouragement wouldn't go astray.
A touch of motivation would be better.

Underachiever.
That's me.
Maybe I'll just pass and shut them up.
Three grade A's and they'd just criticise my choice of career
and tell me that I could do better.

Underachiever?

That's me.

Steven Hyland

TO FLY ALONE

A dark, empty room,
Full. Yet empty;
No life, no soul, no character.
Bits of me stuck to walls;
My life, my friends, my happy times,
But still desperate feelings of nothingness.

Is this how it is?
To grow up and fly?
Solitude, isolation, loneliness
And yet surrounded by people.
A suffocating darkness that surrounds;
Muffling and stifling - a great grey blanket.

Then, a whole in the weave;
A snippet of light, a glance at the world.
Liberating light, resuscitating air
The chance to live, rather than exist
This is how it is.
To grow up and fly.
Fly high.

Carla Maxted

GUTTERSNIPER

The huddled, creased, bin bag of bones is woken by hunger,
drunk with fatigue he closes his eyes to erase the memory of days
gone by.
The sun rises, its bright light revealing his dirty face,
ashamed he hangs his head and studies the cracks in the pavement.
The empty pot between his feet tells him his next meal is days away,
while his screaming stomach tells him it was days ago when he
last ate.
The town begins to bustle as the shops open their doors and the better
people go in,
With a look of despair on his face he watches them squander money
all day long.
Children quicken up their pace as they walk by, some speak
'What's that mummy?'
His head hangs lower - a thing on it, identity is lost with dignity.
He watches women buy themselves new shoes, new dresses, new hats,
and then cross the street to avoid his pitiful state
The day draws to a close and the people slowly go home,
while he stays, watching, waiting, wanting a home, wanting love.
The man in the yellow van comes to sweep up people's
rubbish and food,
while ensuring he doesn't mistake the bundle of rags for something
only fit to burn.
The bundle of rags shivers frequently as the sun hides itself from him
The horror of the night ahead arrives as the moon stares blankly
at the bin bag of bones.

Steven Lowndes

My Star

It haunts me every day and in every dream at night,
As my mind begins to travel from your shore;
if our lives differentiate and separate our paths
Will you still think of me as you did before?
Can I cope with the painful fate
That you will love many that I do not know?
Will their mere presence replace what I was
or will you carry my name to your grave as you go?
Will you watch me get married with pride but regret?
And come to my last bed with fruit and flowers;
And your extra sensual presence to remind me of our youth,
As I live once again in my dying hours.

As you bless centre stage and take on the world
Will I be there as the voice in your song?
When I lay down to rest will I sleep easy?
I never want to wake up and face that you're gone.

Ruth Oakley

FEMININE ANOREXIC

She stands in front of the mirror and cries,
and as the tears fall softly down her face
she sighs.
Watching a shape that's not her own it hits
her with a force beyond hunger
to herself she looks into the heart, but she
sees only a stranger
it kills her to allow the slightest fall.
She would like to be able to fight and
stand tall
but to the others she feels big and so
small
almost a physical hate she has to
consume
instead she collapses in an empty room
her wrists like twigs, no belly, her face
so drawn.

Starved to the extent she wished she'd
never been born
A tear falls down with every stomach rumble
and yet she would die just to feel humble.
People disagree, still she sees lies
but she feels better every time her
stomach cries.

Kelly-Louise Spark

THE PINS ARE DRAWN DEEPER IN

He has the knack for needles
stuck through his arm,
injectionate.
And under the flesh,
the pulling muscles that scream,
there lies a straight patch
to the heart:
and to feeling-deepening.
I am a call for sensation-cessation.
And I am losing,
all weeping and tears
like blood-drops,
drawn from the pool -
there is so little left;
so little breathing left to be done.
The pins are drawn deeper in,
all covered in matt-red,
and matt-brown,
and stickiness.
You are a voodoo doll,
and killing us.
I am awake,
and suffering.

James A H Godden

ANOTHER BOMB, ANOTHER LIFE. WHO CARES?

Another bomb, another life,
Who cares?
Wonder what it's like to die?
glass lies on the ground, shattered,
Mingling with twisted metal.
People have different ideas of peace.

The walking wounded wander aimlessly,
The light of hope extinguished by bitterness,
Looking forward into a black void,
Filled with anger,
Hate that feeds on life
And violence that gorges on it.

Emma Harvey

THE TWELFTH OF JULY

Starlit night, summer's breeze:
The two lovers stand on the beach.
I see them from a distance;
Watch the young man reach
To touch his lover's face.
He smiles and laughs as he
Confesses his love. Kissing his hand
And nose; she smiles. Entwined,
They sink into soft, warm sand
And whisper until dawn.

Lorna Dargan

NOT ABOUT HEROES

She threw away the young lives
on her wasted mission drive.
She stole the promised futures
of the vibrant and alive.
Sent hundreds of innocent young men
to fight her war in foreign lands
She should have begged forgiveness,
but she wants a show of hands.
Our history's more tainted now,
as a nation it's harder to grow
'Cos we're still living in the aftermath
of one woman's huge ego.
What she did can't be undone,
we're still stuck in the dirt that she ploughed.
Still trying to fix the mess she left,
trying to see sky through the cloud.
To my mind it's worse she was female,
as we've been treated like shit for years,
So she should've known what it felt like
to have no-one care for your tears.
As a human she showed no compassion,
as a leader she showed no remorse.
We should have seen how hard-hearted she was,
should've known it was par for the course.
Even though she's no longer the leader,
she's still pulling the strings from behind
And the puppets still act out her 'vision',
twisting our lives and controlling our minds.

Donna Branch

FRIENDS

Friends are friends forever,
Especially when you're down,
Some people just don't understand,
My friends that are all around.

Just where would we be,
Without a shoulder to cry on,
Or someone to make you laugh,
Everyone needs friends,
So don't go putting us down.

If you try to split us up,
Our friendship will survive,
If your friend's a true friend,
They'll sure stick by your side.

Friendship will last forever,
No matter the distance apart,
Whether it's across the ocean,
Or even just next door.

A friend's a friend forever,
No matter what you've done,
A friend is there for you,
Just as you are for them.

All I have to say is,
Don't try to split us up,
Because friends are friends forever,
And that's how it's going to stay.

Emma Williams

FEELINGS

Pain always gives other people gains.

Trust is just another crust.

Everyone is mortified.

But who cares about the score.

You don't need to know,
because I can't exhibit the correct attitude.

I conclude trust is unjust.

Denese Fuller

BUI-DOI

('Conceived in Hell and born in strife')

Your seed is growing.
Your green fingers
Have planted seedlings all round this town

And now they rise,
Sticky with American sap.

The stars and stripes in their eyes
Are denied
By the poverty in which they grow;
Real as trees,
Disowned as bastards.

Your green gloves hang
in the shed
And now you prune a wealthier plant.
Our wealth misinterpreted
Our soil war-leached.

Your children are growing.
American traits
Belie their gullible mothers, and
they wilt.
That sticky sap

Attracts scorn

Like flies.

Jenny Salisbury

HOPEFUL BLUE

New eyes skim blue.
Echoing me,
So I echo you.
You tell me when is
my strawberry time,
You see my studded body.
Not the jagged girl
who sheds a pretty story.
Her pretty obscurity,
Innocence as a freak.
She breathes in my corner,
Playing hide and speak.
You can't tune in
So her words are dry
And tears a little dim.
Dark night colours
Reveal my moon and stars
But she's still here
Touching black glass bars.
We're walking on baby feet
Did you know?
We're just a tiny whisper,
Still in utero.
Will you dive the blue?
And see me,
Sense my fire,
Make it something new.
Still words straddle my tongue,
I know we are together,
Break the glass
And scream my blue forever.

Samantha Wheatley

HEARTACHE

I sit here alone, oh so alone,
No-one can hear me weep or moan.
The sun at the window,
The dark in my eyes,
Just waiting for the ring on the telephone line.

Oh should I phone him,
Oh do I dare?
Why is my love always so unfair?
But through all this suffering and heartbreak I bare,
is it love that I'm meant to find,
Deep down in my heart somewhere?

The tears in my eyes turn to tears of the rain,
As it pelts at the window letting out all my pain,
Oh will he phone me?
Should I write a letter?
No I'll dump him,
I'll find someone better!

Kirsty L Walsh

YOUNG CONFUSION

Our generation young and confused
which path to take in life
carrying weapons pull out a knife
Hazy nights
Bright lights
forget it all in one night
Party hard and fast
enjoy, raise a glass
mind full of air
can't think, don't care.
Wait till it's light
when the time's right
then I'll decide
and stop this ride
Just one more go
as I'm feeling low
then I'll know
which way to go.

Sarah Bull

ICE AND INSANITY

Time is the enemy of all
All on our world
Perhaps on others
Only because time brings change
No-one cares for change
Change brings the unknown
The unknown is feared by all
Human fear of death is but nothing compared to
Uncertainty
Life and death
Have no meaning nor beginning
Unless there is youth
Yet what is youth without
Old age, the last stop before oblivion
Unless . . .
Resurrection awaits
Each of us and to
Die is not to cease to exist but to
Enter the world of the spirit
And yet there remains the fear that there is just
Death, the grim reaper.

Joseph Prince

FAILURE

'You're gonna fail.'
'You're gonna *fail.*'
'You're going to *fail.*'
'You are going to fail.'

It eats at my confidence,
Tears at my pride
Till I have none left,
I just want to hide

Lower, lower, lower
The marks gradually fall.
I'm supposed to get better, not worse;
Failing's no good at all.

It will hold me back,
postpone my career,
That's if I ever get one.
'Failures? We don't employ them here.'

Maybe I should work
That little bit more,
To up my grades
So I pass for sure.

Just don't keep on
Shouting 'failure' at me,
I will work in my own time,
Just wait and you'll see.

Anika Vrettos

YOUTH TODAY

I hope and pray,
That I'll be safe and OK,
If I wake the next day,
Because as a youth today,
We live life in the most horrid way.

Babies being kidnapped,
Children being raped,
Kids overdosing.
Teenagers being murdered.
Spending childhood in prison.
Schoolgirls getting pregnant.
Youngsters dying from AIDS and diseases.

This is our world each and every day,
So I'm glad I woke up today,
And I pray for the next day,
As I have one thing to say,
Must we continue our lives this way?

Lorraine Bell

LIVES

Lives seem perfect.
The reality?
Hidden like faces at a masquerade ball.
Dreams and ideas tossed aside,
Crumpled like paper with too many mistakes.

People live their lives, there but not noticed,
Looking without seeing,
Following without faith.
Drifting and floating like feathers lost by a bird;
Never settling.

Lives seem perfect.
The truth?
Hidden by lies made by ourselves for ourselves.
Love and trust discarded and forgotten,
Left to rot like the last orange nobody wants at the bottom of
the fruit bowl.

People live their lives, there but not noticed,
Racing on but never reaching,
Together yet alone.
Each world as important as the next,
The whole as insignificant as a fleck of dust.
Wind, as soft as a blown kiss, shatters all.

Jessica Bland

THOUGHTS

Young am I, only young
Such burdens I face, I hope I am strong.

Some days I sit and contemplate
of whether I'm free or bound to fate

I think of future, present and past
Time so timeless time so vast

All I see is obscured with choice
I scream in frustration with soundless voice

So many things to think about
Pain, suffering, famine and drought

Happiness, laughter, love and joy
The birth of a child, a girl or a boy

Things that are wrong, things that are right
Things within reach and those out of sight

Where I am now where I will go
All that I have and all that I know

I believe in God I ask myself why
Because I truly believe or am I scared to deny

Shall paradise on Earth really be seen
Or do I need to follow an unreal dream

But then what is wrong with a dream unreal
If it helps a wounded soul to heal

In infinite time I could barely start
To tell all the things I feel in my heart

And this poem you read may seem not much
But for me it is like a healer's touch

That takes my worries for a while
And allows this lifeless face to smile

Then serenity draws like a curtain of night
To slow my heart and blind my sight

To all thoughts, all but one
That total peace will eventually come.

Young am I, only young
Such burdens, I face, I know I am strong.

Paul Cliff

A Young Person Living In The Nineties: Nothing Is What It Seems Anymore . . .

Molecules of water
Collected over the sun-kissed mountain top
Earth and sky mingled in a frenzy of sunlight.
Freshly dewed grass sparkled in the spill
of the sunlight which caressed
Mother Earth with tendrils of warmth.
Trees bowed their heads to kiss
the scattered ashes collected in furrows.
The wind offered a light breeze
Which fondled and aroused
the long blades of grass which decorated
the countryside.

. . . . personification of a dragon,
nothing is what it seems anymore.

Deborah Forster

DYING FOR WAR

Now darkness has taken the land,
Vision crumbles to sand,
Running in desperate despair,
Death drags you to his lair,

Killing fire raining down from crimson skies,
Eyes that once saw truth are glazed with lies,

Hounds of sabbocracy,
Destroy democracy,
Stygian desire for more,
Fuel the fires of war,

Ray of ragged light,
Decapitated the statue of liberty,
Without pity: a single scything glance,
Free-will lost its last chance,

Now freedom is taken by storm,
And blood on their hands will run warm,
Symbols of peace killed by the warlords,

Now war rapes pacifism,
Upon the five point table,
While love a murdered fable,
Is hung from hatred's gable,

Power has stalked the city of light,
By its tread it has brought us night,
Gone is the star of morning,
Our future has passed with a last desperate warning.

Laura Craig

WHEN I GROW UP?

When I grow up, I used to say, I'll get myself a job,
Easy hours, and lots of fun, to bring in a few bob,
A house, a garden, and a car, a holiday each year,
A treasured husband of my own, some children to hold dear.
I had it all so neatly planned, I had my life mapped out,
Never then expecting that I would have cause to doubt,
That the world would ever be around, when I reached adult days,
It's still a possibility if we don't change our ways.
I wonder where we're heading now the world's in such decline,
When stories from our parents now no longer fit our time,
It's just a generation, but our lives cannot compare,
And I just stand and watch our world sinking beyond repair,
War torn countries ripped apart, people maimed and killed,
Adults arming children and then using them as shields,
Half the world is starving while the rest lives on in greed,
Only thinking of themselves and not for others' needs,
Our seas and air polluted, our forests now cut down,
The polar caps are melting, so maybe we'll all drown,
The ozone's disappearing, and then there's acid rain,
Animals near extinction, with only us to blame,
With cancers, AIDS, and CJD and flu that just won't go,
Government nuclear testing? Well how are we to know?
There's children who now murder, hold-ups using guns,
Drug addicts, prostitution, joy riders out for fun,
Paedophiles and rapists, and so the list goes on,
And when I look at where we are, to where we have come from,
To hear them call this progress, how is their moral health?
Not that I can say a lot - a teenage mum myself,
My son is five years old now, and when all is said and done,
When I grow up, all that I want's a future for my son.

Debbie Neal

SEARCHING FOR COMPASSION IN EMPTINESS

The want to leave, it comes and goes,
The need for love, it grows and grows.

To belong, but yet to still be free,
To have the courage to be just me.

A deeper feeling that cannot be found,
A longing for someone to understand.

I want so much to be complete,
Surely there is some way myself can meet.

Alison Snelling

Here We Go Again

I spied you for another moment today.
You hit me quick like a locust wind,
Electric charges through my veins,
That old guitar sequence that kills me.

Every spare thought is of you.
I have this need tonight.
My conscience has just freed me,
But my body won't release me;
Seized my tongue, paralysed my smile.
How will you ever know?

I am afraid to look at you, in case I find,
an empty pocket that the dream's left behind.
Never spoken, never talked, you hamper the
thoughts that protect me.
You shimmer behind my eyes.
The barrier has lifted, and you're still swimming
in my mind.
My control is slipping fast. Here we go again.

Jacqueline A Maguire

PROGRESS

One lady attends to her pampered children.
A young boy is begging for rice.
The lady goes to her concerts, galas, and balls.
The boy is working to eat - working, and dreaming.

When he is older the lady's friend asks him
To come to a private little party.
He looks at his clothes and at his home.
He will not be going to any party.

His children run around with bare feet,
Oblivious to the world that surrounds them.
And what type of world is it? A world where
There is Progress, they say - Progress and Freedom.

His mother dresses him for work,
A tear falling from her eye.
He is not rich or supposedly 'well-educated'.
But she is happy anyway, she thinks.

Children starve, there is waste and want.
A few think the world is Bliss,
That people are happy on their rice fields
And green cricket pitches and warm beer.

For the people of the world have Freedom.
Freedom to starve, to suffer,
To endure pain and punishment.
Making a toy for their children:
Building - building without bricks.

Sarabjit Singh

PARANOIA

'I am a frenetic,
Electric child.
But there's nothing
New on the planet.'

All strangeness had passed.
My organic dreams were left stained by my affluent past.
We spoke only in dark elusive tones, committing nothing.
Committed to nothing.
Condemnation fell from the sky like charity from the elders.

'Leave me alone
All ye who possess.
Leave me be,
Ye who haunts.'

The night was dark and eclectic,
We took sweet shelter in the comfortable horror of side-shows.
Numb with calm, I see the beauty of a thousand faces
In yours.
Removed and in your company . . .

'The night was dark
And I was dead;
I poured sullen mercy
On your head.'

Tom Allen

ALONE

Alone in the world, hidden from view,
scared and frightened of being true.
Alone in every sense there can be,
wishing somebody would find the key.
Lost like a needle in a haystack,
wanting to be found and given back.
Lost like a child on the street,
searching ground for room to place my feet.

Closed to the world and all inside,
wanting to rebel, yet forced to abide.
Closed like the door to my heart;
poked so much and then torn apart.
Trapped like Rapunzel in the tower,
to escape though, lacking will power.
Trapped out there on a deserted island,
needing nothing more than the occasional hand.

Afraid of what tomorrow will bring,
of those that look so tame but sting.
Afraid of what people will say,
censoring thoughts and keeping them at bay.
Hoping that better things will come,
and of those things, I'll have some.
Hoping that things don't go downhill,
not that they can, you can't get lower than nil.

Sonal H Gadhia

HOMELESS

No-one knows his name,
No-one cares,
Rummaging through litter,
Hoping to ease the hunger pain.

As life awakes in the town,
He settles on the hard path,
Hat by feet, harmonica in hand,
But all he receives is a frown.

The river of people glide by,
Occasionally change finds his hat,
Which is still virtually empty,
But he continues to try.

The air is an ocean of sound,
Although none flows to him,
People slowly drift away,
As evening comes around.

Shops will not serve him,
As if he is not human,
Nor animal,
They treat him like a thing.

He settles in a shop doorway,
The cold now creeps over him,
Penetrating his clothes,
He slowly drifts away.

One of many gone,
killed by society,
No funeral, no grave,
Isn't something wrong?

Danny Johnson

FREEDOM

Some say freedom is just for the bird
But with some persuasion you can be lured
Those chains that tie you in knots
They cut your skin and bruise you lots
Every link in those chains that lock you in
Account for every single sin
No matter how big or small
You can't build yourself a wall
Your sins will catch you up in time
They arise all in one line
They join to form that one last chain
That wraps you up in all your pain
However will your freedom live?
Time runs through your fingers like a sieve.
You *will* regret all this one day
In every single living way
And no way will you break that chain
So that you may be as free as a bird again.

Katie Roberts

LOVE IN THE '90s

What love now is.
Safe as houses?
'90s love has
Made me quit.

Like micro-chips,
Waif-models' hips,
(Gone to their lips)
It's shrunk to fit.

We are made to
Choose the menu
Set for us. Do
What we're told.

Rubber first go,
Until we know
What the tests show.
Love's gone cold.

Now the fashion
Is for ration.
Where's the passion
Of the young?

What love now is.
Safe as houses?
'90s love has
All gone wrong.

Coral Lawson

5.30 PM LONDON

We are:
The voracious cluster in the corner,
The caustic strangers without remorse,
With the intoxicating flush of our breath and our minds,
Our whiplash eyes.

We, as three are strong . . .
And young,
And brave,
In glitter-wrap packaging and sequin shells
To reflect the radiance of ourselves.
The hazy force-field shields away the past,
The dust,
The gloom.
While the sprightly sleek and glossy drift towards us . . .
We are happy.

Jenny Poole

GROW UP

Oh, what is it to be a young adult today,
Going through education with no money to pay.
'Spending all your money on a Friday night,
You're only children, make something of your life.'
Oh, how we try to get on, in our time,
College, university or sign on the dotted line.
No jobs to go to, no houses to spare,
Do you really think that we don't care?
Labelling us layabouts, hooligans, drugies and tarts,
Give a dog a bad name and we'll play our parts.
The picture may look poor, the news always bad,
Burglars, muggers and rapists, we're not all that sad,
We like to have fun and a laugh, that's not deviant
So next time you think like that, try and be lenient.
With all the misery and poverty around us right now,
How are we supposed to change, go on, tell me, how?
You think we are going through a stage of relaxation
But we are all mixed up and full of frustration.
I wish you could see the world from a young adult's mind
Deprivation and sorrow, I think you'll find.
But through all this we can still laugh and smile
Because we can go out with our friends and party in style.
This side of life is much better and lighter,
But, I hope, when my kids grow up, their future is brighter.

Emma Staggs

RUNAWAY ROCKET

Crouched on my doorstep,
Against a clear night,
The industry glimmers,
Beautiful, yet all-consuming;
Flames rise bright in the dark,
Like flares of distress;
Lights flash,
And like a picture show
I see a future, flickering,
Shapes smooth, metallic, elegant
But void of life,
Great structures, risen from the ground,
Looming, the epitomes of a human desire
To move forward, forward, into
Territories unknown,
Brave? No, a desire too strong,
A runaway rocket,
Accelerating, without direction,
Not controlled, controlling,
Moving forward, unstoppable.

Neill Waters

HISTORY DONATES

Gunpowder starburst on the faces of foreigners,
On news entertainment television feasting on fears,
Democracy has become festeringly reliant on advertising,
With unhuman beings bred to ignore time passing,
Information war - the profit makers against intelligence,
Turns to find themselves facing crisis of conscience,
And decision haunts with the spirits of consequence.

The ancient world beneath American TV psychology,
Hiding like churchmen plotting the death of theology,
Watching the rebirth of moral-based violence in the discordant,
Benefit rich business sickened at the sight of the penance reliant,
Human life broken and rules by the drug from a wire,
A corporation union co-operates in an enemy desire,
A thousand years of knowledge alight, a world's realm on fire.

Sean Robbins

No-One

Fated.
Lethal slaughter.
The name of
Daughter,
Washed from your
Bloody hands.
You cause no
Pain,
Or begging shame,
For I have won
In the stakes of
Life.
Away, and free,
From the name
Of duty.
I will worry
No more, or even
Say your name.
I am not
To blame.

Georgia Lee Brittain

THE SPECTRAL ROOM

Delve into a sphere of sounds,
Floating in a pool of voices.
Rushing,
Flowing,
Beating,
Sensing mutual ambience under the air.

Nocturnal vibrations shake dawn's light.

Waltz in

Fall back and wander,
Until the night burns out.

Dazed comprehension between
Realms of reality.
Sense aside the colourful light,
Then walk in new thoughts.

Keith Rawcliffe

Inner Sanctuary

The sun is sieved through my net curtains
and is scattered across my page as
I write.
The white net curtain strung up
In front of the window - and its negative,
Cast over my face, my hand, my page.

The music plays . . .

Peering out from behind the dark knotted
strands of jet which have fallen
Into a veil beyond my face -
I can see you . . . but you can't see me.

The music is dark and crawls through me
like smudged charcoal, running mascara
- Black -
Angelic.
Sweetly, painfully haunting.

It makes me feel filthy, radiantly, deliciously
Filthy.
My head looks down but my eyes look
Up.
Up at the sun - but it can't touch me.
It tries.

Outside it has distorted my mop of strands
and blow-torched them brown.
But inside -
In here it's black and it can't touch my
Face anymore.
It's safe in here . . . I think I'll stay . . . ?

Yasmin Huda

THE JOURNEY OF ADOLESCENCE

As I stumble blindly through my teenage years,
I hear voices cautioning me.
I never listen.
Revelling in the delights of youth,
It seems like eternity belongs to me.
Youth means so many things:
A cloudless sky; an unspoilt beach,
The innocence of a pure love.
I tend to forget, in my glee,
Those who are less fortunate than myself.

Yet, across the oceans,
There is a different view of adolescence.
A boy in a poor village,
Begs for food,
For if he should stop,
He would not survive another day.
In his language, the word 'hope' doesn't exist,
Third world poverty is all he knows.
Yet, throughout his poor existence,
He has never lost the ability to smile.
He looks at the same cloudless sunny sky with shining eyes,
And he sees the whole world as beautiful.

Georgina Ann Price

BAD NEWS

Silence fell over the room
like a blanket on a fire,
both cold and hurt
was wallowing round
Tears were never to tire.
The scene of faces all in pain
were hard to even bare,
the fact of the matter
even now could never be compared.
All sad, tired and full of hate,
that a person they cared
had suffered in fate.
I can never forget the
laughter you gave,
your face so full,
a smile so brave.

C Mann

THE TIGER

Our eyes meet.
I feel your pain,
Your sorrow,
Your burning desire
For freedom.
I see you as you should be,
A predator
Beautiful and
Deadly,
A killer
Stalking your prey,
Powerful and proud.
Here, confined in your cell,
Life imprisonment
Attaches to no crime.
Our eyes meet.
I understand.
And in my mind
I set you free.

Rhian Blackmore

HIDDEN GENDER

What lies beneath that beer-swilling, masculine exterior?
A lipstick, powder and painted beauty, clawing to escape
From the prison of your conscience.
She's diseasing your mind,
Screeching to be set free,
Yet still you keep her chained within.
Ten years on and it's too late.
Driven to distraction by her monotonous wailing,
You shall both die, insane beings.
Everyone will ask themselves,
'Why didn't he open up and reveal that hidden gender?'

Georgina Pearce

THE KISS

Shadows envelop their bodies
as they move towards one another
open hearts and arms
welcoming each other in.

The surrounding walls seal in their love
The clouds of apprehension disappear
and the bright knowledge of requited love
flows freely into their bodies

Their eyes interlocked with each other
Their bodies turned in acceptance
Her emery hair tumbles down her shoulders
as his hands steady her body

The serenity of the moment takes hold
as her arms cling to his for support
The moment closes in, a last lingering
The embrace of a lifetime - a kiss.

Georgina Macey

PLEASE SAY HE WILL

Will the scars ever go away?
Will the bruises ever fade?
Will he ever not be angry?
Please say he will.

Will I ever get away?
Will I ever have the courage?
Will he ever stop drinking?
Please say he will

Will the words ever cease to hurt?
Will I ever do anything right?
Will he ever love me?
Please say he will

Will he ever stop hurting me?
Will he ever stop hating me?
Will he ever know I love him?
Please say he will.

Lynda Beveridge

LOVE IS . . .

In a world that's so confused inside,
What is love?

Is it family? Is it the church?
Or is it the husband, that's left his family in the lurch?
Is it the date, that ended in rape?
Or was it the murder in our estate?

Is love, what this nation consists of?
Is there love, in our criminal justice?
Is love the bomb, in which hundreds were killed?
Is love sold in the night-club pill?

Is love when innocent children are tossed out in the streets?
With no-one that they can turn to, and no place to sleep.
Is love when they're raped and set on fire?
Is it love, when we watch and not desire;
not desire to respond, to a nation's cry for love.

Love is patient, love is kind,
Love is always finding time.
Time for others before ourselves,
time to heal and time to help.
Time to show that we do care
Time to reach out and be aware;
be aware of a nation's cry,
a cry for love.

Love can be found both in you and me,
If you dig down deep enough, love is surely what you see.
Take that love, but don't keep it for yourself,
give it to others,
so that we may be, a nation full of love!

Rhonda Norris

MY HORRID LIFE

All year round is the same old thing
Winter autumn summer and spring.

I'll sit in a corner most of the time
because this is the only home of mine.

Each morning I'll wake up,
The weather is freezing
I'll be tossing and turning
coughing and sneezing.

People walking by, throwing me money
little kids laughing thinking it's funny.

People look at me as if I'm dirt
not even thinking I get hurt.

I am a person
I am alone
The only difference is, I have no home

But for me it's my life
it's the same old things
Because this is what, my horrid life brings.

Hayley Kent

UNTITLED

I find myself thrown away from you,
Upwards,
Away.

I clutch at the clouds,
As my eyes swim between the blues,
Alight and innocent.

I soar with her in my hands,
Through the wisps and cottons,
The hues and awe,
Never so at peace.

If you tear me away I shall return,
If you drag me down I will fight your grasp,
Never have I been so alone as with her,
And never so fulfilled.

And I hear her words over,
A solitary voice in my mind,
As she sings to me . . .

'Do not bring us down with your fears and your cries,
Up here you cannot touch us,
Up here we are free,
Up here we are alive . . . '

Omar Khan

THE GLADE

I stand upon the path of ancient wisdom,
Within the glade of the ancient trees.
Here I lie - from true death hidden -
Here my aching heart at ease.

Within this bower - this glade of love -
Where the messengers of angels' wings above
Sing their songs of hope and glee,
Their admonitions to all below -
Without this glade of inner-glow -
Tell of an ever-nearing prophecy.

So seek not the towering citadels
Of darkness and mammon -
The cities of the damned -
But come I beg within the holy glade,
A step away from the promised land.

Theo Vasilis

THE GAME

His falsities chilled my bleeding heart,
And I knew by that heavy coldness
He had bought her as a conquest.
My friend had been the pawn
In his game.
I had lost, so had she.

Her beauty and goodness
Expelled from within, her
Happiness touched, warmed others
With a single momentary smile.
How had he accessed her?
How in hell had he changed her?

His burnt orange hair echoed
My hatred, her forthcoming pain.
He couldn't claim her totally,
But how much damage
Would he inflict, and at
What cost?

She no longer laughed, as she had,
Just sat holding his orange phone
Pretending to be the old model
While he spoke with a foul mouth.
Everyone noticed the change, passively
Hating him, feeling sorry for her.

Fate took pity,
A six month trip to escape
The tightening hold.
She would find her true self, until
She came back
To reclaim his dying love.

Adam Wilson

EVERY MINUTE SO PRECIOUS

Every minute so precious
But is it really true?
Let me enlighten you
Those who try to hold on
Not to let go
Who feel time is running low
Before time even had began

Those that can only live in the past
Re-playing those memories
Who refuse to let things change
They're wrong
Don't dwell on time
Don't try to hold on
Take my advice

Just live.

H A M

LADY NIGHT

Heavenly mist hung like a widow's veil,
Seductive night covered the sleeping land;
Then came an alluring voice through the dale
A graceful shadow reaching out a hand,
Her rolling hair like the azure skies,
Her complexion fair as the rising moon.
Exotic mistress behind all men's closed eyes
A smile in harmony with night's tune,
Quintessential love for her dark mystery,
Brings solace to the mundane life of man;
A thousand galaxies fall at her knee
To love her is only as mortals can,
Her long desired form transcends the night,
When her nemesis dawn, brings infernal light.

J L Machon

REGRET

She regrets it all,
At first she was having a ball.
But now the clocks have changed,
Everything seems deranged.
She made the mistake, now feels the ache.
She takes all the abuse, but there is no excuse.
It should not have all happened, she wants it to end
and for her and the boy to be just good friends.
She has to live with the guilt, with the feeling to wilt.
Knowing what she has done,
All things have begun, to appear to be true,
If only she knew,
of the consequences of her actions, and of her emotions.
She is left with the pain, with nothing to gain.
And now she regrets, the risks she had set,
for falling in love,
with what she thought was the dove
of her life causing much strife.
She has all the time to mourn, but soon it will dawn
onto what she had done.
It may have been fun,
at first for the thirst, of an eagerness burst.
She holds her head low and wants no-one to know,
About the mistake she had made;
Hoping the memories will fade.

Kim Goddard

LIFE ON EARTH

Life on earth is hell,
only when we die
we go to a better place.
Our existence is a challenge,
or maybe a test
to be first in the race.
But the devil comes and
the people are evil
just to get their own way;
they would steal, fight
cause death and wars
to be big in life today.
This is all wrong.
Life should be peaceful
full of friendship and
love.
but while so much hate
remains,
only the good will get sent
above.

Esther Stone

SURVIVAL

Our everyday
Here
In this prison - circle
Floats
Wanders blindly
Not knowing
Not seeing
The road ahead.

Our every footstep -
A journey to
The unknown.
Every second -
A breath lost.
Fate's silent touch -
An invisible cut.
Our every thought -
A mystery in themselves.

Like the fire - sun
Our pain will live -
A piece of the puzzle
Forever present,
The strength of our
Survival.

Distant cries
Ageing faces
Are our
Only hope
For an eternal rest,
Our only path
Into the stillness of life.

Natalie Robinson

THE WORLD

I look out of my window and what
do I see,

A world full of hate, how can this
be?

I see children dying and firing
guns,

Death and suffering a world come
undone

The age of technology, the world
is alive,

So why do I see panic and fear by
my side?

The world is a struggle, a fight
to survive, our neighbouring
countries fighting to thrive.

I look out of my window and what
do I see,

A world that's been ruined by you
and by me.

Alison Rann

ECHO BEACH

Echo beach, far away in time.
Dusty, wind-swept shores,
nothing but the cry of creaking gulls,
haunting the pale blue sky.
Perhaps the loneliest place in the world,
belonging to me in its own quiet way.
The salt air has now gone.
Echo beach, so far away in time.

Jamie Borley

FACILE ORIGIN

From our mothers we fall,
like rusty dripping oil
We are all force fed strychnine
To corrupt our minds with moral ideals.

Part of the master race,
So liberal and free,
This I know is blackness,
That is suffocating me,

We are all here,
Laughing in the pools of freedom,
But we are really drowning,
Just drowning like all the rest.

J Harvey

THE REJECTION

The utter despair overwhelmed her whole body,
And as her hands dropped loosely down
the book which she held,
Collapsed
Covering her face.
I didn't have to see the tears, they were audible
and her entire body shook
with total desolation
At the horribleness of the situation.
The tension hung thickly about the room.
There was no comfort I could give to her.
No words to calm her jangled nerves.
I could only flee that terrible room, hoping
she would recover in privacy.
            Hope
had left her for that while and with it went
any sense of self-esteem and worth.
Her predicament smelt like the decaying rot, which no doubt she felt
enveloping her.
And I
Could do nothing,
But watch.
I dared not look into her eyes, nor even toward her,
For fear
Of losing the tears which were readily lining my own eyes.

No brave faces were put on.
Although the ego boosting talk did come
it was much later.
When we could all comprehend such luxuries as happiness did exist.

Parneet Purewal

THE MOURN SHORES

The Mourn Shores hit me like a beating heart.
Crashing solemnly, as a distinctive momento.
When the tide leaves, the heart turns cold.
Whilst petty trinkets are sprawled in view to comfort me.
But the Mourn Shores will always resume,
For we have young hearts, which will be seldomly touched.
Throughout our eroding shore lines.
Preparing up for the unknown, and the unwanted.

Sarah Watkins

OLDER AND WISER

At first it all seems different,
Different to before,
All the things that used to fit,
Don't fit anymore.

You don't seem to enjoy,
The things you did before,
Remember when you were always reassured,
You don't need that anymore.

People who you thought you knew,
You never really knew before,
And all those important things,
Don't seem to matter anymore.

All those people seem to fade,
And they don't talk to you anymore,
Then with relief you realise,
You're more grown up than before.

Helen Roberts

No More Dreams

I wanted to live life,

Make a difference,
Give, not take.

But 'maturity' beckons,
I'm dragged, nails scraping, to a soul wrenching future.

A future which isn't mine,
A one way future,
9 to 5.

A future where the only love is of power
and the only icon, money.

My future is inevitable.
Soon I'll be stained and standardised
like the people I despise the most.

Andy Peppin

WHAT IS LOVE?

I'll tell you today what love is,
What do you think it is?
Well I'll tell you today anyway.
Love is the floating aroma around us,
Love is in the air,
Love is what we live on,
It is the inner power within us,
and we all bear it, for life is nothing without love.
You want to cry when your loved one is not near,
or when your only love has left you.
But I say, *love*, is the greatest love of all,
which lies deep inside your heart and soul, safe from all.
Love is when you feel pain inside your heart,
longing for your loved one to be beside you,
and of all, love is two hearts becoming one,
where the fear of life or death doesn't break that bond.
This for me is love, do you realise?
But then again who am I to talk about love?
When my loved one has taken away my heart from me,
by a distance seeming eternity.
I live in hope, that one day I will be able to relive that love
once again, that right now is so far away from me.
But for now, I explain to others what love is.

Minu Lathar

EMPTY STAGE

I was sitting on a seat in the theatre
The other day - it doesn't matter when -
And I was watching my life falling by.
I couldn't leave, although I wanted to,
Even though there was nothing to see.
The spotlights were dim,
And the actors were gone,
But still I waited, alone in the dark,
Always hoping that at any moment,
Someone would enter,
And fill up the scene.
Finally somebody did come, and stayed a while.
She enchanted my eyes, clawed at my attention,
and touched my heart with happiness.
Then when her lines were done,
She left me, as quickly as she appeared.
Everything went dark again,
And again I waited, in silent agony,
For someone to come and fill
The empty stage which was my life.

David Thomas

FOR THE SAKE OF TOMORROW, TODAY

I remember a day, when I could play
With children of any race.
But now, my dear, I don't know where
Exactly was that place.

I remember a day alas, when I could look out of glass,
And see all life breathing free.
'Without a mask?' my dearest asked,
'Where on earth could that be?'

I remember, too, when the cup was blue
Filled with clouds; she was protection
But now she's dead, leaving a ghastly red,
Destroyed by a nucleic destruction.

I remember a time, when the world was mine,
And I could fondle my Mother's nature.
'The doves and seagulls? But wasn't it illegal?
Weren't they the essentials for the future?'

I stroked my dearest, whose expression was fiercest,
'Take me there I want see, this place so wild, so far and free!'
My eyes turned to sorrow, we never thought of tomorrow,
And how their lives would be.

My dear, it is all in the past, when we thought peace would last,
50 long years before.
Evil was up to its tricks, now is 2046,
We must build our lives once more.

Get the priorities straight, don't leave it too late,
Be sure it's great for your generation
I hang my head low, and if I knew then, what I now know,
I would have changed the thoughts of the nation.

Nishma J Patel

LOVE

Our bodies moist and damp
As the beads of sweat did roll
Upon the very brows
Which had held the frowns so cold
My hands caressed your body
How soft your skin does feel
You whispered that you loved me
My heart it then did seal
The times it had been broken
They were forgotten now
I gave to you my token
And oath to you my vow
The token I gave was love
The vow was never pain
I hope you understood how much
I would never hurt you again
As you held me in your arms
Our hearts did beat as one
And now I want to tell you
You're the one I truly love
You're very special to me
And I'm never going to leave
There is just one thing I would like you to know
You are the wind beneath my wings.

Caroline Croker

LIFE

One day you feel normal
The next you feel a lost cause
Why can't anyone help you?
The day draws to a close

The pain strikes again and again
You are drawn to suffer in silence
But what do you gain by feeling this way
You are denying yourself of your presence

You ask yourself questions
Why me? Did I do something wrong?
Nevertheless life goes on
You are becoming strong.

Elizabeth Keller

ARTFUL PASSION

Skilfully, the slick-haired expert
Caressed her slender neck,
Smoothly, casually, his dry fingers
Scaled; unfaltering down from her head.

He held her body
Close to his, steadying her
In his warm embrace,
Resting his arm on her side.

He whispered inaudible words
Absently, leaning over her,
To watch his fingers dance
Upon her milky white body.

In perfect mathematical accuracy,
He motioned closer to her head,
His left hand virtually around her neck,
Now sweating, he relaxed,
And smiled in self-satisfaction.

He glanced at the clock,
Realising he had been with her
For three whole hours; he said nothing,
But as he struck the final chord,
The Don Juan of music
Laid her gently down against her amplifier.

Stephen Bonnar

NEW EYES

Illuminance is all knowing
The way youth always goes
Understanding and in control
On the path it chose
Independence conceived loneliness
When darkness came along to see
Brushed aside; forgotten about
Light trying to break free
Shadows came to stand the fight
Of jealousy struggling inside
Security and warmth until
Access to love was denied
Voids born of shadows
Shadows brought despair
Darkness engulfed everything
Truth was laid to bare:
Illuminance knows not the ways
Of where the path will lead
Hurt, lost, confused and alone
Left to reap its own seeds.

Gemma Unit

The River Flows On

As the river gently flows,
Around the bends that take
Her to her destiny.
I too travel to mine,
My destiny I do not know.

As she erupts into vigorous rapids
Speeds up and nears the fall,
I quickly slip away from
The things I love so much.

The water tumbles downwards
Majestically plummets to a pool,
I clumsily try to hang on
To the edge of my existence.

The river still flows on
And I too am taking breaths.

Anwen Terry

ESCAPISM

Summer, warm and mellow,
evening sunlight
filtering through oak leaves,
illuminating the mossy clearing,
gilding the woodbine.
Spiders' webs shimmered with rainbows
in pools of golden sunlight.

There I built my refuge,
one final, defiant
act of childhood.

I worked in the forest,
dragging branches.
My friends worked in hotels,
gift shops, cafes, making money.

Bark on skin,
moss underfoot,
saw slung over my shoulder
ball of string in hand,
whistling as I explored
rocks, clearings, bush and briar.

I built my leafy room,
supported in the arms
of a growing oak.
A shrine to youth,
nature and happiness.

But I had to desert the effort
long before it was finished.
I haven't been back since.

Seran Dolma

Our World

If I could turn back time
I'd set out to remind
All the people of the world
Love one another
Sister and brother
Join hands
Together we can make the world a better place
And save ourselves
From fallen grace

They say we started with a bang
Well I don't want it to end as we began
Look after this world as we only have one
It's not as if we could trade it in
Once it's lost its glitzy appeal and fun
War, starvation, poverty, racism, prejudice, sexism . . .
Does this list never end?
Don't make them your enemies
Make them your friend!

Rachel Bourner

TINY LIGHTS

We arrive late -
I catch a glimpse of you through the doorway.
Then I don't see you again until you're on stage.
I'm not even sure if you've noticed us.

When you get up to sing
You glance up and smile
Dedicate that song to us
And I fall in love with you again.

At the end, you come over and speak to us -
Your first greeting sends chills down my spine.
I can only smile and nod.
We drive home.

Tiny lights in the distance, your voice coming from the radio.
Me smiling as the darkness closes in.

Paula Clancy

I Can Do It On My Own

I'm early in my years, no education,
no job and pregnant,
I thought he would stand by,
he left me when I told him,
oh God how he made me cry.

They all said get rid or put it up
for adoption,
but I am going to have my baby,
because I do have the option.

Who cares if he has left me,
who cares if I'm on my own,
I'm going to be a good mother and I'll
nurse her till she's grown.

I'll manage through the ups and downs,
I'll manage through the pain,
I'm going to be there for my baby,
through the wind and snow and rain.

Can't you see I don't need you,
I can do this by myself,
and when she's feeling poorly I can nurse
her back to health.

I'll make sure she has all she needs,
and she's clever when she's grown.
I don't need your help,
I can do it on my own.

Amanda-Jayne Weir

SHINY PAPER BAG

Her whole being smells of smoke;
sticky smoke
wrapped up in its shiny paper bag,
with the dream inside.
And I can taste the drinks and cigarettes
stuck to my throat and head.

But this dream is someone else
to be something other
a taste through different eyes
in its shiny paper bag.

High in the head
she sings herself to sleep.
She will have her dream
in the paper bag.
And you leave with her soul
stolen while she sleeps,
beneath the paper bag.

The songs fail with the stars,
the dream remains in the paper bag -
she goes to the grey sky
in her smoke filled clothes,
a bag slung over her shoulder
with someone's dream inside.

R Moran

I HAVE A CHOICE

I have a choice.
I can choose to do drugs,
I can choose to smoke,
I can choose to be an alcoholic,
I can choose to be a nobody.

Or I can choose to do something with my life.
I could be a lawyer, a nurse, a teacher, a fireman.
I can choose to make the most of my assets,
To set myself a goal in life and do my utmost to achieve it.

I can choose to disregard people's feelings,
Or I can choose to respect them.

I can choose to be a considerate person,
Or I can choose to be someone that nobody really likes.

I can choose to like my family
And I can choose to like myself.

This is the 1990s
and I have a choice.

Joanne Hocken

DIVIDE LINES DRAWN

Look to the green of the leaves and a deep blue sky,
A scarlet fire, seen through a silver eye;
Look next to a child's mind, all of love and nursery rhyme,
Before humanity's hand batters him blind;
Filling him with propaganda hate and a driving distaste
For all that is simple and sure, a miracle cure, but now, it is too late.

A flaccid life, a plastic wife, a materialistic glow,
He is sailing safely through the waves and
Stealing flowers from a thousand graves,
Making the most of his monetary libido.

j
Filling a Sunday read with fallacial greed, still they lie,
And laying blame with an empty claim, still they die,
Tossing a token gesture for others' pleasure but still they fight.

These little graduate men, pushing a birthday pen,
A concrete office in a concrete city,
Slippery saloon exhausting monoxide pity,
While plastic wives furnish homes with hides,
Victims of 'civility's' countless crimes.

Money makes the world go round,
Even nature concedes and gives up ground,
Savannah to sand, man flaying a nature hand,
Sparrow's song and the sunset gold, we find them sold.
Dying in a dream makes for a sweaty sleep;
Here in the rising heat, Earth is growing cold.

Andrew Jackson

DAMASK

Damask, is the colour of the red, red, rose,
Which you threw down at your feet when you left me.
Damask, is the heightened hue of your cheeks as you again rejected
my love.
Damask, is the fire of passion that burns in my breast,
For you, and you alone.
Damask, is the gentle light of the sky at dawn,
And the birds that sing in it, telling the world just how much
I love you.
Damask, became your fear, as you fled from my anger,
And I ran after you, and followed you silently home.
Damask, is the colour of your blood, as it drip, drip, drips,
on the floor,
Forming a pool, just like a looking-glass,
Damask are your lips, trying to sound out alarm,
While your roving eyes stare into mine, searching for
some explanation.
Damask, became my sorrow, when the cold light of day fell onto you
once more,
And your lifeless body lay there on the stone floor.

Kim Wilkinson

INTELLIGENCE

Intelligence is the key
But from time to time
it is the enemy.

Positive advancement it can give
to anyone who engages
with it,
however,
lose control and let intelligence
dictate to you, then intelligence
is negative retardation.

The positive effects aspects gained
are shifted and the
view is altered. A new
dimension to the
straight up, straight down.

Cynicism, advantage, power, calculation corrupt.
Intelligence is these. Power corrupts,
absolute power corrupts absolutely,
but you have to be intelligent to corrupt.

Nothing and nowhere
are achieved unless intelligence is in
accompaniment.

Slowly, inching, festering, worming
its way to wherever it wants to get to.
I cannot tell where it has come from
or where it is going,
but who can stop it?

It can take you from
agony to exultation,
from the abyss to ecstasy,
a roaming free radical
able to
inflict or influence at the speed of light.
Back for good, or not?

R G Barratt

TEARDROPS

Today he met the girl of his dreams,
If only she was his,
War and peace wouldn't separate them.

He'd give her flowers,
Show his affections towards her,
But she's not an object of desire.

I know they'd be great,
If they had a chance,
To give their love a try.

The quiet boy at the back,
Has teardrops falling from his eyes,
and heart.

Brett Sadler

BIRTHDAY POEM

So ridiculously happy
it is a sentence to recall
or anger perhaps,
        that you are winning.

The thin salt taste that slips
back my voiceless throat
releases two bitter barbs,
to run furious free,
        How prophetic these are.

And as for your indulgent riddles!
This locked horizon is screaming to you.
Listen.
I could depend
        grow
           profess.

What force pushes inside this green that
cushions all our bodies' falls
attentively crawls the marked veins
of my hand, as turning a curl,
the sun's heat begins to mend.
And I would serve open all senses
to this honest artless nature,

yet, to touch you is a guilty confession.
Crude in its new-born state. Untamed.
Repulsively hawking for air, ugly is its form.
Yet how astounding its conception
I know to covet,
the beauty I see.

So ridiculously full of height
had I plunged the platform
of the sky and not fall harmed
but as with wings
not north south east find,
more your hidden eyes' direction.

So this day, you possessed my imagination.

H S Trompeteler

MY FRIEND

Because we are friends
There is not a price
That can be planted upon our friendship.
A friendship like ours cannot be measured;
Or bought with money . . . or even promises.
To me, it is wonderful in itself;
The feelings of closeness and regard
                          that we share.
Our friendship will forever be a
                          part of my life.
And although I don't say it all of the time -
Perhaps this is good -
For if it was said everyday,
It would not mean as much as it does
At this moment in time.

Ann Murray

FACES
Auschwitz 1996

The earth and trees cried uncontrollably.
The air held her breath for fear of
Disturbing the resting.
How could she breath whilst
Others were forced to be so silent.
The walls ached as if trying to express
What they had seen and heard.
The earth could still feel the bodies
Spread across its surface.
I dreaded to touch the stones,
For I was afraid they may release
The screams they had absorbed.
The sun shone but did not warm
Where its beams touched.
There was nothing to be warmed,
For hope had died long ago.
My mind still adds to the scenes
And I cannot bare the sight.
I close my eyes and they become more vivid,
Those faces, oh, those faces!
I am forced to listen,
For the story is not told by sound.
A word need not be said,
For words could not express.
There is an anger within me,
Not at an individual or a nation,
But at fact and at the human nature
Which created the fear
Upon those faces, oh, those faces.

Rachel Veerman

THE DREAM AMID HOPELESSNESS

An adult one morning you realise,
In the war and poverty stricken world
We are powerless to halt
Destruction, the hateful and absolute destruction.
What's the point?
Why should I try to change it?
No, instead we wallow in a mire of self pity
And the world sinks further into murky despair.
- It's hopeless.

We dream sweet, wonderful dreams,
Love, peace and happiness surrounds.
The Utopia we all crave
Birds happy in the clear sky,
Fish in the crystal river,
The sun-drenched golden meadow, the rolling hills.
Each person content and loved.

But dream is all we do,
No-one helps to change,
Life becomes quickly a mere existence.
We soon accept and become hardened,
We forget to follow the dream,
It's seen as hopeless
But, even there, if we can see it
- Hope exists.

Roisin Spence

GAZING

Look to the night my friends!
Look and seek out the stars!
In them find ourselves,
Points of light, shining outwards,
Braving an infinite nothingness,
Only to be obscured by wispy clouds
As we are obscured by pettiness;
Potential lost, unattainable heights.

Now let us ride the tail of the comet,
On its majestic course of creation'
In that find our way of living:
All moving on one bleak circle
With no end and no escape,
Only a continuous daily trudge,
Glamour and joy only bygones.

In the stars we might find the answers,
To those questions never asked,
To those problems never solved,
We have no hope of finding them here
In this prison we have made of Earth;
Only the icy comfort of bigotry and hate,
Serving our wants and needs.

And few have the inclination to care
And fewer would want to know,
Of the real importance of living
And the real need to care for life.

For most have nothing to wish upon
Save the ashes of stars once burning,
And the remnants of hope once alive.

David Ford

CHILD OF THE 90S

Death disease famine war drugs terrorism
The child of the 90s suffers.
This is the world that we live in
'Oh the youth of today, the youth of today'
That's all I ever hear.
'It wasn't like this in my day, you know, the good old days'
Well if these days of yours were so wonderful
Why are we left with such an uncaring society?
Built on war and hardship.
What do you expect from us living in the society that you created?
A society based on your generation of killers, addicts and glorified
military murderers.
If these are our only role models then how are we supposed to act?
But hear this; don't tar us with the brush of the few,
You were our age once.
Society changed, if you don't like it that's tough
There are those of us out there who strive for the good
We haven't had our impact on the future yet.
So when you start preaching, about the youth of today,
just remember this . . .
We're living the legacy of your youth.

Rebekah Reynolds

ALBA

May my path be good or evil
I seek to address it not
for my indifference of gumption
Excitement becomes a deep dark blot

So yes you're quite welcome to
come on home.
Stop shouting
I'd rather walk quietly alone

Thought I cannot see my way
it's not a statement without thought
I won't tell you my doubts
And yet I seek to hide them not

So, no there's no way for any of us to
Freely roam
Stooped crouching
Passively still I wonder about home.

David Gale

HALF KID, HALF 'GROWN UP'

I'm 19 years old,
or is it 19 years young?
I can be adult,
yet still have fun!

I'm searching for a home,
for my boyfriend and me,
I should be serious,
but it's such a novelty.

I love being 'off my 'ead',
and dancing till I drop.
yet I can't wait to do things,
like our 'weekly shop'.

I was at Uni,
looking forward to messing about.
But it went wrong - I didn't like it,
and so I dropped out.

So I'm swanning around,
With my mature attitude,
but still feeling naive,
and a little confused.

I'm sometimes called a woman,
when I feel like a girl, instead.
I'm half kid, half 'grown-up',
With one dizzy teenage head.

Tamsin Wick

FROM THE DARKNESS

Those first, sharp, fingers of light,
Encircle, ensnare and entrap.
Prising me from you.
Scything those bonds that hold us,
The feelings, fancies and fears,
That linked and entwined us,
Are now cut down.
Laid waste with the cold clarity of the day,
Stripped of all restraint,
Thoughts are marshalled,
Desires quelled.
Only with the dark is it stilled
Clasped and cradled,
Calmed with the musk of emotions,
Liberated by the night.
Until dawn seals the mask,
And a mind is once more halved.

Stephen Coulson

HOLIDAY

I want to tell you
how your love makes me feel
like a diver who finds his pearl
when his lungs
are beating his body for air.

I want to tell you
how my love is
a hidden cave
in the labyrinth of my heart
dark - until you walked in.

The words crowd onto my tongue
like shoppers
on the first day of the sales
but the doors are already closed.
(and they stay outside,
their purpose betrayed)

And so my love remains
like a man in Inverness
waiting for a bus
on a bank holiday.

Elaine Jackson

EIGHTEEN

Eighteen sure is a funny age;
To a child it seems so old,
To the world I'm now a grown up
An adult, mature and bold.

But, I don't feel a grown up,
For seventeen years I've been a child,
Not ready to face the real world.
Now past problems seems so mild.

At school, life seems so complicated
Full of ups and downs.
I used to think things got better -
But eighteen's as bad as it sounds.

I'm not sure what I want from life.
Too much pressure to decide.
Peers, family, teachers, friends
Can't see it from my side.

Where do I want to go in life?
How can I gain control?
Should I go for everything
To reach my long term goal?

A job or off to Uni?
Decisions I've got to make.
Bewildering confusion
Controls which path to take.

But despite confusion, despair and grief,
There's one certainty for sure,
In four months and twenty-seven days exact,
I'll be this age no more!

Karen Jane Gledhill

In Conversation With . . .
(After Bergman)

Across the oaken barricade,
Seated,
Faceless narcissus,
Shrouded in putrefied hemp.
Reaping tool glistening.
(Spotlight)

Dance the tarantella,
Pagan rite
Under boughs and branches.
Syth-like,
Now arms of family tree.

'Who'll win chess?'
Questions.
'How many d'ya kill in the war?'
'Granddaddy?'
Blackout.

Black sockets,
Staring through
Narcissus, faceless.
'How many d'ya kill?
'How many will I?'

Michael Jones

NATURAL

Plastic girls
With peroxide curls
With their mucked up insides
Seeking nutrition
Which is not accommodated in a size 6 figure.

Endless needs
Of those on the front pages of all the magazines
Those who glide down catwalks
The 20th century IT girls and their bottomless make-up bags
Speaking rehearsed words to an enthralled public

What happened to being yourself
With our naked faces
Are natural smiles
Wearing our own high-street styles

What happened to being natural
Was it the media
Or the guy who's the multi-millionaire
Well they'll have to excuse me
My figure, what I wear
My concern for life
Instead of moaning at Jesus Christ, 'cause my lipstick
is the wrong shade
or my skirt's not the appropriate length in the fashion mogul's eyes.

I am what I am
I wear what I wear
I have the choice the freedom
The right to the polite ignorance of 20th century's dictated
luxurious necessities
Invented for those too blind to see
Life is for living
it may not be artificial enough for publicity
But it's the one of experience, money can't buy.

Clair Walker

Time's Safe Keeper

Shallow under ancient parts,
Where none shall stir,
And none shall go,
Old, asleep, 1000 years,
Devoured by time's safe keeper.

Safe the undiscovered joy,
Of what to find,
And who to know,
1000 years shall pass once more,
Devoured by time's safe keeper.

Mystery such treasure holds,
Unknown to any kind but those,
Who passed away those years ago,
1000 old forgotten souls,
Devoured by time's safe keeper.

Colleen Nunn

IN MEMORIUM FOR GOOD TIMES PAST

Once the sighs and tears and byes have gone,
The laughs, the love and the joy lives on.
The past is thought of, and tomorrow comes,
Yesterdays joining so the futures rise,
Crescendoing to life and light again.

So, come walk in the lanes,
As the memories play,
To be joined by greater and brighter days.
Let your friendships colour earth and sky,
For the coming tomorrows and returning yesterdays.

James Dale

DOUBLE GLAZING, MOBILE PHONES AND GOD

I don't remember reading
A chapter of that name in
The Good Book
And when, after six days' hard work
God had finished the world
I don't recall
Receiving a call from the man in the sky
Telling me to come and have a look.
I live in a house, which has windows
Which I look through
Upon God's achievement, and I
Have no desire for any more
And when I'm in the cinema
I do not wish to hear your mobile phone,
Portable ego, selling us
The myth of your popularity.

Jennie Hodgson

THE BEST YEARS OF MY LIFE?

It's a different world here - new
People, places, thoughts.
Feelings emerge that I never knew were there,
Memories keep me grasping at what is gone.

Home is in the past. Sixth-form,
Homework's, school trips - the old way of life.
This is different. Vast and imposing, intimidating and
Nerve-racking. This is university.

I've reached the next stage in my life.
Shouts of 'Good-bye!,' 'Good-luck!,'
'They'll be the best years of your life'
Penetrate into my thoughts.

I'm still waiting.

Alexandra McNulty

THE STRANGER INSIDE

One disaster after the other,
That's what you produce.
Guilty stomach churning feelings
Are endless when you rise.

Who are you to bring such shamefulness,
That life has been given?
I wonder if you mean it;
Or are, yourself, ordained.

Who is you master?
Are you your own?
A unit that we cannot govern;
Make us party to your own sick shows.

Sometimes I lack you
And am happy and calm.
Suddenly you take control
And, simply, disaster comes.

I desire to understand you,
For you're unpredictable as hell.
I long to control you;
Truly make life my own.
The future can never be kneaded
With your strength in our souls.

Jane Strongman

MIDNIGHT

When it snowed last Thursday afternoon
On my way home, marching along,
Hiding from the world in my sheltering hood,
My hands pressing moulds into my pockets,
I thought of you.
How you'd tell me that
'Atmospheric vapour frozen into ice crystals
Are falling to earth in light white flakes.'

But I know that if those magic,
Baby clouds had stroked your cheek,
Transforming into tears as they met the heat,
That you'd have understood,
Like a child understands Christmas -
Really, impulsively, shallowly but truly.

I thought too about how I,
Wrapped up in my green duffle coat,
Tied with my white scarf,
Sealed by red gloves,
Would have felt naked - baby exposed
By your charm,
Thrilling as a lighted tree in a dark room,
My hand drawn to yours
As it once was to my mother's.

Maybe we can ignore it now,
Shrug it off like a foolish fairytale.
But last Thursday afternoon
Was one of those transforming times
When sense is suspended . . .
More can happen when it's
White outside and red inside.

Rachael Owens

New Year

I stand here so powerless
As the rotted year dies fast
I don't want to see another one born -
It only speaks of the last.

The starving still die helplessly
As war adds to the dead
And government pity won't buy them grain
And speeches don't bring bread.

And class still hates equality
And fire of race burns bright
With whip and gun and necklace -
Black opposing white.

Politicians' blatant lies
Crooked deals that pay
Just ensure public distraction
Before election day.

And AIDS steals yet more victims
'Kiss of death' from 'kiss of life'
And streets are tight with murder, rape
With sleeping pill and knife.

Another poisoned year lies dead
As whisky and song flow free
I don't want another year born, if it
Can only mean this to me.

Catherine Mair

YOUNG MOTHERS OF THE 90's

Everywhere I go people stop to glare,
Some in disbelief or those who want to stare.
I keep on pushing my baby along,
In crowds they whisper she's a bit young.

I sit to feed my child so sweet,
People come up to me to watch her eat,
'You're so young' they say,
'Just how do you cope? All those responsibilities.'
People comment old and young,
'I bet it is hard being a single mum,
Struggling alone can't be much fun.'

People make rude comments about this generation,
Young mums the topic of conversation.
I sit I ponder what do they know,
I'm not single I'm married you know!

Rachel Watson

HIGH TIDE

Children ripple into vision,
Balloons rising skywards,
Smiles, fat and floating,
Sandcastles digging on the beach.
All this was theirs to play with;
Your wrinkles a rope to skip,
Eyes a safe pool to paddle in,
Silver hair a cliff to climb
To the height of emotion.
Stroking the sand like a memory,
Waves wash the time away.

Anna Warrington

THE 3AM BLUES
(Or come down when everyone else is asleep!)

Hallway timber croaks
Like an ancient ship.
Wall clocks mark each
Thunderous second.
My stomach holds a
Drag race.
The inevitable faucet
Drops tidal waves.
Bathroom door becomes
Train crash.
Bathroom light the
Insolent sun - glaring
Beneath sleeping doors.
Buzzing refrigerator
Hums, redundant in
A swarm of
Drumming,
3am
Silence!

Jenny Evans

A RADICALLY ALTERNATIVE ENVIRONMENTAL SONG
(In the style of Monty Python)

(Speaking:)
The physics of the Earth seems to defy a lot of people,
And they all forget that Ice Age many many years ago.
We had a rather cold spell in the middle eighteen-hundreds,
Now we're simply warming up again - I'll tell you what I know . . .

(Singing:)
Those melting polar ice caps are indeed a rather rare sight -
It just happened that the continents lined up in the right way.
The warm Atlantic gulf stream cannot get up to the North pole,
And in the South we have a largish land-mass made of clay.

Our orbit round the sun is quite distinctly not a circle
And it changes all the time you know - it's really quite unstable,
Sometimes nearer, sometimes farther, in a longish sort of cycle
So complaints of global warming are quite simply just a fable.

The water level of the sea is changing as it always has
The fossil records show that this has nowt to do with us:
It's all to do with continents and wobbles in our orbit,
So don't go blaming CO_2, it's not worth all the fuss.

The human race is capable of being too big-headed.
We think that we can save The World - I'd rather stay in bed;
We only have the power to save *our*selves from extinction,
So maybe we could all work out how to do *that* instead!

Oliver Humpage

THE WORLD AND ITS LEADERS

What kind of a world do we live in?
stop for a second and think.

Everyone begins to scream,
as they hear bullets fired into the air.

Innocent bodies are scattered upon the ground,
the atmosphere is filled with no love or warmth.

When the war is finished,
there's nothing, but silence.

As devastation spreads across the world, like a large explosion,
leaders still refuse to see what they're doing is wrong.

This raging and rioting of wars today,
has trapped innocent people as victims.

Day after day they hear more bombs explode,
as more enemies emerge from nowhere.

As loving and as hateful as we are,
these people are human, and deserve to be treated better.

So really, it's time to realise that this world was made for all of us,
and we should share it with each other.

Elizabeth Campbell

MIND RIDDLING

Loved him, loving them . . . but did I or do I?

Crush for him, crush on him, crush on them,
God I'm sick of crushing!
One billion, trillion thoughts through my head
Tom was handsome, Dick was sweet and Harry always dresses neat.
But who cares? They still couldn't handle my love.
I could put it down to maturity or insanity or . . .
Oh God! Will somebody stop my *mind riddling*?

Nicole Hughes

PLACE

You stand behind the glass
watching the line trundle past,
One breaks away and the mocks and jeers
push them further out,
Until they are surrounded by themselves,
And no one can touch them.
Their words stain your mind,
And the fear of isolation compels you to join,
As you march towards conformity.
Indifferent to everything
And nothing.
The line suppresses your voice,
And the strength to look away,
As you become one of them.
Controlled by the unseen force,
Of the majority.

Yvette Smith

BIRD BOY

I see you
A mass of dark and light wiggly lines
And I no longer
Know you
We are very separate
And I find the capacity not to like you
I see you from another angle stranger.
In this I lose my thin threads
Like sticky spider webs
And I am more alone than ever
More alone
More alone
Than ever.
Yet I look at you and smile
Think of you and lose my mind
I wanted this separation
Because something thick and dark
Told me so.
It painted a picture.
Fly into the sky my bird boy
With golden wings
Let the sun scorch you.
Leave me to my gritted teeth
And pulling chains
And wrenched emotions
Leave me empty and light
Like a beached plastic bottle
Lid opened long before
Liquid flowed away.

Julia Davis

THE BOMB

Forward, backward round and round my whole world
turned upside down.
People running screaming in fear.
Bang! The ground below me violently shakes.
It feels like being dragged backwards through a
massive earthquake.
I look up into utter destruction one bang created
such disruption.
In fear to move I stay lying still
All I hear is the thudding, pounding of my heart.
People running frantic all around
Firemen, police, paramedics attend to people injured
on the ground.
The air is deadly silent, the only noise, a broken alarm.
People, pushing, shoving, trying to move from harm
Other people helping them, trying to keep them calm.
Waiting here in the deserted street being trodden on
by chaotic feet.
Looking around I watch them
As if an enemy has intruded their den.
My limbs feel stiff, my body cold
Is it my time?
I wonder if the lady and dog got away
All those small children, will they see another
day?
Oh! Please help, be on your way
All I remember of that day
Lying there thinking some people are cruel
Aren't they?

Vanessa Clough

ALONE IN TIR NA NOG

Alone in Tir na nOg I strive
For proof that I am still alive
Ensnared by freedom's mythic bliss
A thousand fates succeed the kiss.

That burgeons into something deeper
Wedding bells; or railway sleeper
Broken bodied, broken hearted
Few here would call me 'dear departed'

No Niamh of golden hair awaits
To guide through melancholy straits
To frame insatiable desire
Extract my soul from youth's quagmire.

This voyage is for me alone
And should I fail to make it home
The only truth that shall be clearer
Is - each new dawn brings darkness nearer.

David Rogers

PHANTOM

He is my phantom,
Not of Opera but of life.
He is always there when I talk,
Burning of day or dead of night.

I know not his name.

With pale skin and cold flesh,
He looks almost as real as any man.
But when night casts her esoteric shadow,
He is phantom, he is wolf, he is demon.

Maybe I know what he is?

He comes to me in a dream of fantasy,
Silently calling for my surrender to his might.
His power commands the night and her slaves.
His power commands my life and my death.

Even I now obey him.

Dare I go with him and will I be back?
A choice of life or death.
But with whom shall I live?
And with whom shall I die?

He whispers his dark desire to me.

His seduction of my soul has begun,
Drawing me forever closer to him.
He leads me to a strange dark place.
Never before have I been, and never shall I leave.

I know now his name is Vampyr.

Angela Cook

A REASONABLY CONCISE POEM POINTING OUT THAT ALL TOO OFTEN IT IS THE HUMAN CONDITION TO BE OBSESSED WITH LABELLING THINGS UNNECESSARILY WHEN WE COULD MERELY LEAVE IT TO THEIR BASIC CONTENT TO GIVE US THE ANSWER TO WHAT THEY ARE AND ALSO WHAT THEIR PURPOSE IS

This
Is shorter than the title.

Paul Gamble

WHY?

I'm me, but why me? Why not?
Why not a dark, tragic
Meaningless number, a statistic,
Only recognisable to the few
Who understand that maybe,
Or surely that statistic is us all?

Why is the question often unanswered
Ignored and even feared
Though one's opinions of why
Can be so important in
Unlocking the answers to the
Relevance of any statistic.

Why this blonde hair, these
Blue eyes and other genetic features?
Why this rain, wind and snow
Lashing down on this meaningless stage?
Why could we go on forever
In naming so many irrelevancies?

Have these irrelevancies anything
Beyond their meaningless reasons?
Or have we surrendered to the
Nothing that surrounds us?
Questions unanswered, as do remain
The opinions of why?

Simon Gay

A Whale's Sad Song

Some people say the whales ask to be killed
They swim into the bay
And shout E*at me! Eat me!*
But do they?

The reality is still too cruel
The whales are still all dying
Slowly and in agony
But they still keep on fighting

So many different types of whale
But all reduced to a precious few
We must help to keep them alive
There must be something we can do

Another thing that worries me so
Is the condition whales are kept
In places like *Sea World*
The keepers think they are saving them
But they still all die in the end

Their songs are so beautiful
It's amazing how they make contact
But then we go and ruin it
By the stupid way we act.

This is something I feel strongly about
They have such a beautiful home
We should let them live in peace
Why can't we just leave them alone?

Trudy Sargent

I AM

I am yet, what I am none cares or knows,
My friends forsake me as a memory lost.
I was the self consumer of my problems,
They rose and vanished in oblivious host.

Life shadowed in love's frenzied
And yet I always used to hide.
I hid my love to my despite,
Until I could not bare
The brightness of the light.

Into the living sea of waking dreams
Where there is no sense of life or joy
Apart from the vast wrecks
Of my great respects.
Even the dearest that I loved the best,
Did not show a little sympathy from the rest.

I have had great friends and companions
In my school days,
All, all are gone
Even the beautiful old faces.

M Irfan

FUTURE'S BRIGHT

Today I found my treasure and hid it
Under my head pillow in fearful excitement
Of what could come of my own shaky optimism
Scathed as ever with electricity and foreseeing regret
The end of a crescendo wave
Down a fast moving spiral
This is quick - as time is
Given very little of it,
Further evidence of the dissidence
Felt by those like me from another time
Maybe another place
Our minds never connect with the minutes
The seconds already gone,
So I go headlong into the remains
Forever crying amidst sounds of laughter.

Genneah-Eloise Turner

THIS SUMMER AFTERNOON

As I sit on this bench
on this summer afternoon and close
my eyes, I hear the silence
of the day creeping past on its slow journey.

The sun is beaming down
but it is not a bright day,
the clouds are gathering
in an attempt to overthrow us.

They grow dark and purple,
pregnant with rain,
heavy tense, getting ready
for a battle with the elements

that control us.
On my bench I feel the first
drops of water on my brow.
It has started.

People are rushing indoors
'We must keep dry!'
They cry, but it is their cowardice
that sends them in.

Again the sun has to fight on alone,
one hot soldier, an Achilles
without a heel. The thunder roars
and lightening flashes

Full of anger, full of purpose
meaning to attack and hurt,
but it is not as powerful as the sun.
Again we are saved.

But it will return, twice as angry,
twice as powerful.
As I sit again on this bench
I quietly thank the sun.

Victoria Abbott

RACISM

A step back, forwards -
Dart, stop -
All, new -
Hard, knot -
Black, blood -
Deep, thought -
Dangerous
Falling,
Abstract?
No,
Why always no?
Yes indeed,
Far too posh,
Black not white?
Style,
Gone,
Going though,
Gradually,
Does not matter,
Don't care,
Cry,
Fall,
Hit, the ground,
End.

Sophie Pathan

BOOK OF DAYS

The first chapter ended in heartache.
My soul felt desperately alone, torn apart, broken.
I dropped the book and fumbled in the darkness,
Catching it before the precious script hit the hard stone floor beneath.
Slowing I placed the book on the table, I had lost the page.
I was feeling weary, helpless, so dependent on the security I had lost.
I began to remember as I flipped through the memory filled pages of
     the first chapter.
What I found there made me understand that these ruins of my former
     self
were new foundations for the next chapter in my life.
I lifted the book once again and found the right page, without
     hesitation.
And so chapter two begins and I become enthralled as I witness
     fate wrapping me up
in her silken threads and I see the wonderful tapestry of life spread
     all around.
I know now what type of man is right for me, I think I always knew
     but was side-tracked
He is a true kindred spirit and lays a colourful feast before my starving
soul.
He is a crystal amongst decay, a diamond found in a lump of
     dusty coal.
He is like grey wax still in the unopened tin.
I will have a difficult task opening that tin, it is sealed so tightly.
But once opened I will see that it is easy from then on.
The wax spreads thick at first but then smoothly and easily.
Although it appears dull and grey at first
Eventually it will shine like the sun reflecting on newly polished
     glass.
And so I begin the task of opening the sealed tin.
I hope chapter two ends better than chapter one.

Sinead Kennedy

CLOUD

(For Claire)

Perhaps like a cloud - forever changing?
Soft and gentle - quietly caring?
Watch it high, still it all moves on . . .

It's just a dream to recall. I can't hold on to her heart
I try to rise above it and its cloud.
More I wish it was beside me now.

Marck James

WORLD OF MY DAY

No more peace, no more understanding.
The love that is left is fading,
fading into the night.
The hate for each other is changing,
changing into the dark.

Miriam Burley

QUIET PLACE

I'm going to find me
A clear blue quiet
Somewhere in my head.

I'm going to find me
A clear blue quiet
And take you there instead.

I'll take you to
This simple place
And keep you there with me.

I'll hold you in
My loving arms
And never set you free.

Jo Inkster

REVELATION

One life
One game
One way
I remain
One night
One more time
One desire
Of mine
Spinning around
Spiralling down
A scream of silence
A distant sound
Reaching the ears of angels
Healing hands break the spell

A revelation
In sight
One choice
It's black and white
One hill
Ahead
Or one pit
Leading down to the depths
Falling down
To my knees
One prayer
I find my feet
I catch my breath
As I run
To my destiny
To my heaven.

Andrea Smith

PALATE OF CONFUSION

And it was then, I think,
that I really saw,
caught a glimpse of
what it was all about.
The colours blurring
yet so vividly clear.
The most prominent was red,
a brilliant, burning red
that could have been so beautiful
were it not as direct as blood.
And the green invading,
permeating all like a dye
that has to be scrubbed away,
naturally entailing pain.
And the yellow, for some reason,
but most of all the purple;
ambivalent, sad, bold but
so obstinately indecisive.
A sure, marked shade of
cowardice, evasiveness, fear.
Why? Why? A million times, why?
Reasons slipping through the fingers,
explanations hiding away, afraid of discovery.
Perhaps that is what we are doing,
mere bit players in a
dazzling, bright light show.
And the colours that blind us.
Frighten us, confuse us, make us aware.

Simon Walsh

DEPRESSION

Sometimes I feel the pit I've dug is so deep
I'll never get out.
Trapped in my abyss, no one can hear me if
I scream or if I shout.

I feel that somewhere long ago I
discarded the golden key.
That would open my heart, release my
mind and truly make me free.

I've searched in my own caverns, tried
to make myself be happy.
Instead I'm always irritable, depressed
and very snappy.

Why do I feel worthless, an insignificant
blot?
I wish I could understand and untie
all the knots.

I've contemplated suicide, not a sober
thought.
I'm not going to give up searching, not
going to end up caught.

Two steps forward, one step back is
better than none at all.
One day I'll find what I'm looking for of
that you can be sure.

I always blame myself for anything
that's bad.
Always looking on the black side, I
sometimes think I'm mad.

The more I think and wonder, the
more confused I get.
But I haven't finished living,
the fight's not over yet.

K Messer

OWLS

Comes an owl in the darkness,
the darkness split with stars,
comes another, comes another,
one across the other,
in darkness from afar.

So
we found ourselves together,
one against the other,
fearing for the light.

Was it she who sang to me,
we were owls, we were owls,
owls in the night.

Robert Langston

YOU

You make me smile.
A warm glow beaming within;
Listening to your voice
and joking with you.
But most;
Most I wish I could
Spread that warmth to you
and hug you,
squeeze you
and be wrapped up in your big embrace.
I want to see you smile,
Tingle with a burning warmth,
To stroke your face,
Smooth your eyebrows,
Entwine my fingers in your hair,
Kiss your nose,
Cuddle up within your arms.
Just be with you.

Rachael Kriefman

CHARITY

People are living in fear
They're starving in the third world
People are dying from disease
There are people living on the streets in the cold and wet

They all need our help
They're not asking for much
A few pence
A couple of minutes a week
It's not much to ask.

They just want to live their lives their way
To stand on their own two feet
Without fear of diseases or going hungry.

Richard Wade

GROWING UP

Everyone thinks that growing up is easy,
Well, I say it's not,
You have so little time to take things in,
And you have to learn a lot!

Firstly there is the opposite sex,
They are so confusing to me,
They say one thing and mean another,
It's pointless, don't you agree?

Then there is education, jobs and money,
You can't survive without these three,
You need a job to have money,
And education gives you the key.

When you are growing up, times can get tough,
But don't ever give in,
Just keep on pushing and growing,
and eventually you will win.

J Satherley

LIFE

I had such high hopes when I was young
My life would be perfect and loads of fun
I'd have a family, someone to love and a job
I'd have no reason to frown or to sob.

While growing older I realised how hard it can be
Trying to please others, never pleasing me
So much competition and pressure to be the best
You were teased if you were different from the rest.

Wrong or right - so many turnings to take
Yes or no - too many decisions to make
New emotions like anger, sorrow and pain
Will my life ever be the same again?

Now as an adult through different eyes I see
Life doesn't always turn out how you'd like it to be
If the decision or turning you make goes wrong
Hold your head high, try again, hold on.

Treat your life carefully it's the only one you've got
Live it to the full, try and enjoy it a lot
Confidence, strength and hope is the way
For a life you will love day after day.

Nicola Ireland

THIS IS MY HOME

So you've come to view my home,
Well let me show you around.
Just the one room as you can see,
Room for one, cosy for me.
Sturdy walls the two boxes have,
Only the best, and they were free.
It's got good insulation,
Decorated with newsprint,
Well, it makes a good read!
Running water no less,
But only when it rains,
And that happens often out hear, believe me.
Fully furnished too . . .
Carpeted with a blanket, no less, what a luxury
Heating? Of course and light too.
All environmentally friendly, with a little help from the sun
When it shines, which isn't often, believe me.
Yes, wide doors too, it's not too draughty
As long as the wind doesn't blow too strongly.
Yes, it is a very large garden isn't it,
But the public are forever wanting to come and see it too.
I think that's all I can show you
There's nothing else to see
It's not much I know
But remember . . .
Those two boxes
And the newspapers that fly free
That's home for me.

Nichola Kinnersley

A HOPEFUL SOUL

Unconsciously we pass them by,
Their damaged souls shed across our feet;
Invisible to the selfish eye,
Unheard of, just a dark and lonely street.

Unaware of lost love and pain,
Their hearts spilling over an empty gutter;
To them it is all but a chosen game,
The same old words they religiously mutter.

Uncared for by majority,
Their faces stare into another world;
Pleading awareness and not for pity,
Comforted once again by surrounding cold.

Unwillingly we sigh and give,
Their cries echoing and shattering time;
Hope is their only reason to live -
Today it rains, but beyond it may shine.

Dianne Lister

DEPTH

Depth.
Acquiring a certain depth,
So I sit here my mind a cotton field,
A windy day, no calm, no hush.
I search for a certain depth,
That would satisfy my reach,
I tickle a soothing notion, I will acquire.
But the digging bleeds my fingers.
Blackened blood dirtying my fingers.
How can I make blood red,
And cotton clean?
How, ever, to indulge in the peace of pure.
I yearn for a soothing notion,
I will acquire.

Aamna Khokhar

SHRINE

Since you left, two years ago, your room has remained untouched.
The floor is strewn with battered books and yellowing papers,
Crooked posters with crumple-torn corners adorn the walls,
And a collection of limescaled mugs, confined within their dust
      marked territories, eagerly await your return.
Sometimes I feel compelled to sit and stare through the dirt-encrusted
      window panes,
Envision the world through your eyes;
Red and tear stained.
The air inside is stale and suffocating;
Half-thoughts and palpable emotions race around between the walls,
Unwilling to escape.
The room has acquired an echo, as if in recognition of your absence,
And the hands of the unwatched clock have frozen, aware of the
      futility of their existence.

Sarah Teichler

PARTY OF ONE

- Mmm . . . good evening garcon (that's French for boy you know),
  table for one?
- Just one! not for two or four? . . . sure?
- No, a table for an odd number, one!

One. 1. Such a simple one, yet such a messy one.
he puts me in the corner, behind the fake, waxy yucca,
Behind the swing door, next to the pile of dirty tablecloths.
Plants, kitchen, laundry . . . all so familiar.
I ask for the *other* chair to be taken,
It's cold, steely presence presents too much of a distraction.

Aurora Leigh, my soul companion. I eat sole meunière,
And read.
A couple turn and peer, as if I had four breasts.
No, not four breasts, just a badly fitting bra.
So, picking up a couple of pommes noisettes (or potato footballs)
  as he used to call them) I launch my attach.
Plop! in her champagne it falls, a substitute strawberry.
I leave, a lady behaving badly, having paid my share of the bill.

Back home alone - for a ménage à une. No need to floss.

Lauren Brennan

JAM

You saturate my mind
Until I am brimming over.
The feelings fall from my lid,
I am full to bursting. No more can I withstand,
Obese with words and feelings
So constricted have they become,
They can no longer escape.
This isn't just a jam it's a blockage.
Air tight-sealed
Air tight-cemented
Nothing is getting through me
Everything is kept inside
No one, nothing else is allowed
in or out.

Charlotte Keates

NEW AMMUNITION

Commitment, not passion -
Has gone out of fashion,
I'm told.

A new ammunition -
To reach your ambition,
Fool's gold.

To step on your neighbour -
Returning the favour,
Ice cold.

Significant other -
An unattached lover,
No hold.

A callous betrayal
Love isn't for sale
For pieces of silver
Weighed out on a scale.

Cathy Bulley

CONCRETE JUNGLE

The day starts for the lives saturated with monotony,
'Rise and shine listeners, it's busy on the roads today,'
Fumbling and fingering,
Trying to silence that damn radio,
Coffee made, shower hot,
'Homelessness on the rise again,'
Would love to help but sorry,
I'm late.

The choreographed journey gains momentum,
A leap in unison along the cold pavement,
An exhibition of neat ties and dry-cleaned Macs,
Assembled at the crossings,
Glaring up at the architects' more eccentric days,
'Yesterday, planning permission was granted.'
Can't build across, must go up, up, up,
Concrete clouds?

Another day at the office drags,
Half dead from a caffeine overdose,
Stay calm, not to worry,
Urban air should do the trick,
A lethargic walk now congregates the now loose ties and heavy Macs,
The city, busy, rushing, racing but tiring,
Obsessive urban rituals,
I love city life.

Lee Flavell

INFORMATION

We hope you have enjoyed reading this book - and that you will continue to enjoy it in the coming years.

If you like reading and writing poetry drop us a line, or give us a call, and we'll send you a free information pack.

Write to :-

StrongWords Information
1-2 Wainman Road
Woodston
Peterborough
PE2 7BU
(01733) 230746